AQUARIUM FISH

A TROPICAL WONDERLAND

With an introduction by Elso Lodi

CRESCENT BOOKS

Contents

3 Foreword
5 Choosing an aquarium
6 Water
7 Preparing the tank floor
  Lighting
8 Temperature
9 Oxygenation
10 Aquatic plants
11 Feeding
  Hygiene
12 Breeding and rearing fry
13 Preventing disease
14 Marine aquariums
15 Index to aquarium fishes illustrated

We thank Enrico Giovenzana for his technical assistance, and the 'Little Zoo' at Milan for specimens kindly placed at our disposal

All the photographs in this volume are by Carlo Bevilacqua
The drawings on pages 6, 8, 9, 10, 12 and 14 are by Rodney Shackell

Translated from the Italian of Elso Lodi

My purpose in writing this book was to try to communicate the keen interest and sense of protection which I feel towards that important part of nature – the underwater world. In our industrial civilisation, rivers and lakes are polluted by waste from our factories and sewage from our over-populated towns and cities. In too many waterways already, life has been irreplaceably destroyed and some species of fish are becoming more and more rare. This bleak situation has been brought about by an almost total lack of respect for all forms of non-human life, but there is perhaps one small crumb of comfort. During recent years interest in tropical fish has greatly increased in the Western world; this educational hobby has become more and more popular and is now financially within the reach of almost everyone. Shops which sell tropical fish are to be found everywhere.

The upkeep of an aquarium need take only a small part of one's leisure hours. One is comfortably installed in front of a well-lit aquarium: the colourful pageant begins. Fascinating and unexpected aspects of fish life unfold themselves before the eyes of the observer. The novice aquarist is permitted to share a secret life lived in an element vastly different from his own. He could be a spectator at the love play of a pair of Siamese Fighting Fish, *Betta splendens*, and discover that the male, so ruthless and bloodthirsty when dispatching a rival, is a kind and attentive father who spends his time tending the fertilised eggs and then the fry (young fish) in a nest of air bubbles.

Where also for so little money and no inconvenience can one forget the noise and frenzy of the world in the street, and lose oneself in this fantastic submarine world where a serene and triumphant Nature writes her own laws and proclaims her own miracles?

Sometimes through ignorance of even the most elementary biological or technological procedures the novice can be unsuccessful and, sadly, the aquarium will be emptied and banished to the cellar, a cupboard or attic. But if he follows carefully the brief but essential instructions found in the following pages the enthusiast will be able not only to set up an aquarium correctly but also to breed his chosen species in captivity and rear the fry. Finally, vivid and detailed colour photographs will enable him to learn to identify the more common tropical fish and to distinguish the peculiar characteristics of each.

Elso Lodi

Choosing an aquarium

For the novice who wants to set up his first aquarium, a tank holding about 20 litres* of water is a good size to start with as it does not require too much attention. Later it can be changed for a larger one and the smaller one used for breeding or quarantining new acquisitions, as will be explained in detail later on.

Aquariums can be of various shapes, but it is advisable to have a rectangular one and not the traditional 'goldfish bowl', since this not only distorts the images of the fish but also prevents a good exchange of oxygen between the surface water and the air.

There are two types of rectangular tank on sale: those with a metal frame and those without. In the former the plate glass is fixed to the frame with special plastic cement; these aquariums are much tougher than other types as their corners are protected by angular metallic corner-pieces and the plate glass is more resistant to shock, as the plastic cement acts as a cushion. If one of the sides gets damaged, it is easily repaired, because only one pane has to be replaced. This type of tank needs great care when it is being filled, particularly at the beginning when the walls have not settled properly and the water seeps between the glass and the cement. As the water level rises, however, the increased water pressure against the inside of the walls causes them to adhere more firmly to the cement so that the seepage gradually diminishes. To speed the operation up tepid water (30°–40°C)** can be used: this softens the cement and manual pressure can be exerted on the inside of the walls where the adhesion is not perfect. Any water seepage at the beginning of the operation quickly diminishes and will cease completely after a couple of hours.

After the aquarium has been filled it is still not ready

* Measurements are given in metric terms. A conversion table appears on page 14.

** Temperatures are given in centigrade degrees. Fahrenheit equivalents are provided in a table on page 14.

for the fish. The water should now be left in the tank on its own for at least a week to allow the toxic substances contained in the cement to dissolve in the water. When this water is changed the filter of algae and the incrustations which have formed on the cement should be left as they are, as they isolate the cement and prevent completely any further decomposition into the water of the substances which it contains. The same precaution should be observed in the periodic cleanings which are a part of normal aquarium maintenance.

The frame can be made of enamelled iron, stainless steel, aluminium, brass, plastic or other material. Stainless steel is unquestionably best from both the esthetic point of view and because it will not rust, but since it costs more, the cheaper enamelled iron is often used, particularly for larger aquariums. For small tanks a plastic frame is acceptable.

So far as tanks without frames are concerned, there is one kind very pleasing to look at: it is made entirely of glass welded with special glues which vary according to the make. It is of course much more delicate than the other kinds and difficult and very expensive to repair if it is partly damaged. Some years ago this kind of tank tended to fall apart suddenly with disastrous consequences, but this tendency has been corrected and the author has used one for a long time and finds it still perfectly watertight. The aquarist who buys it is advised to get a guarantee.

There are now tanks on sale which are made of polyvinyl chloride which do not have the drawbacks mentioned, but they have to be handled carefully to avoid scratches on the walls. Avoid absolutely tanks with zinc bottoms as these dissolve zinc salts into the water, fatal to fish in some concentrations.

For esthetic reasons tanks are often built with a greater depth than width, although from a functional point of view it is better to have a tank almost as wide as it is deep, to allow a free exchange of gases between the water and the surrounding air.

The tank should be provided with a glass cover to

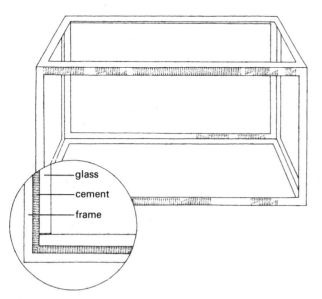

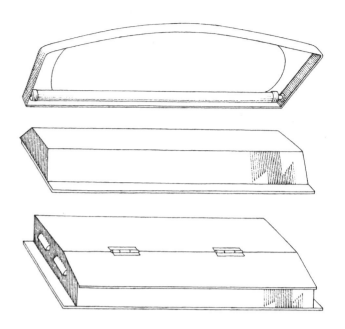

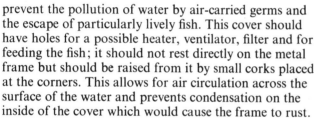

glass

cement

frame

prevent the pollution of water by air-carried germs and the escape of particularly lively fish. This cover should have holes for a possible heater, ventilator, filter and for feeding the fish; it should not rest directly on the metal frame but should be raised from it by small corks placed at the corners. This allows for air circulation across the surface of the water and prevents condensation on the inside of the cover which would cause the frame to rust.

Water

There is no universally ideal water, since different species of fish and plants have different needs. Only where individual fish or plants of the same species or homogeneous group are reared together can the chemical and physical properties of water be modified so as to obtain optimum conditions. But this is of interest only to specialists. Let us examine the properties which average water should have: that is, water which has been modified to suit the greatest number of tropical fish.

Non-polluted water from mountain streams or springs is usually quite suitable for this purpose but it can be difficult to obtain supplies regularly. It is more convenient therefore to use drinking water from municipal sources and modify it as necessary. This water cannot be used straight from the tap because it often contains substances which release chlorine, poisonous to fish. A large receptacle should be filled with the necessary quantity of water and left to 'season' for a week in some clean and sheltered place. It should be covered by a piece of glass raised two or three centimetres to prevent dust falling into the water and polluting it, and to allow the chlorine to escape into the atmosphere as the air circulates. Bacterial flora which would develop abundantly in the presence of fish and plants is also destroyed during this period.

Drinking water is generally rich in calcium and magnesium salts and is, in chemical terms, hard. Many tropical fish live better in softer water which contains smaller quantities of these compounds. The hardness of water is measured as if it were all due to calcium

carbonate (chalk), and the way it is expressed varies in different parts of the world. In France, for example, hardness is expressed as French degrees; one degree of hardness is equal to one part of calcium carbonate dissolved in 100,000 parts of water. In Britain, the English or 'Clark's' degree of hardness is given in grains of calcium carbonate per gallon of water. The United States adopts a similar system except that the US gallon (231 cu in) is smaller than the imperial gallon (277¼ cu in); a correspondingly lower reading is thus obtained. Tap water almost always has over 100 parts per million of calcium carbonate and this is termed 'slightly hard'. Over 200 parts per million is regarded as 'hard' or 'very hard'. The water must be 'softened', for example by diluting it with distilled water: to 10 litres of drinking water is added 5–10 litres of distilled water. A quicker method is to boil part of the water which is being seasoned (50–70 per cent) to cause the precipitation of the calcium carbonate. This is then left to cool and after 8–10 hours the clear water is drained off, leaving the chalky precipitate at the bottom.

In an aquarium which is in use there is continual evaporation and this increases the hardness of the water – which is still further increased if one adds untreated tap water to maintain the level. It is necessary to have a supply of water which does not contain calcium salts and this can be obtained, for example, when the refrigerator is defrosted; rain (collected in a clean receptacle and then boiled) is also suitable, as is very light, non-gaseous mineral water – this last property very important, since carbon dioxide in larger doses than normal will kill the fish. Tap water boiled and poured off (or filtered through filter paper) can be safely used. Another important factor which has to be taken into account is the concentration of free ions of hydrogen, expressed as the pH which shows the alkalinity, neutrality, or acidity of the water. pH has a scale ranging from 0 to 14: neutral solutions have pH 7, acid solutions from 0 to 7 and alkaline solutions from 7 to 14. In the aquarium the pH should be around 6·8 to 7. Noticeable variations will cause

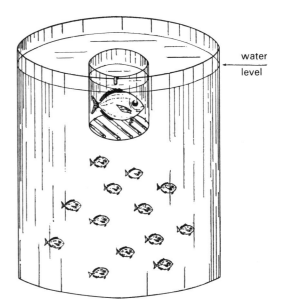

water level

damage to the gills, epidermis, and fins of the fish, and may lead to their death.

Leaving aside precise methods of measuring the pH which need special apparatus, the simplest procedure is to use a paper impregnated with special pH dye indicators which change colour at different values, and a scale of readings from 6 to 8. When these strips of paper are immersed or wetted with two or three drops of water their change of colour indicates the pH of the liquid. This method is less precise but the margin of error is negligible provided that the reading is made immediately the paper strip has been wetted, because shortly afterwards there are variations in colour which alter the value of the reading.

Water which is too acid or too alkaline can be corrected by adding non-toxic acidifiers or alkalisers. As a fundamental rule the correction of the pH factor should be made gradually, and always in 2–5 litres of water drained off from the aquarium and then slowly remixed, avoiding sharp increases or decreases of pH. If the water is acid, bicarbonate of soda is added; if alkaline, acidity may be produced by the use of peat, long-fallen oak or beech leaves or phosphoric or tannic acids, but care must be exercised by the inexperienced chemical users.

Water from an aquarium should never be completely replaced unless it is polluted, because 'old' water lowers the incidence of certain ailments such as white spot or fungal diseases. Moreover, a complete replacement almost inevitably brings a variation of hardness and pH with grave consequences to both fish and plant life.

Preparing the tank floor

The bottom of the tank is lined with a layer several centimetres deep of a mixture of gravel and silica sand. Marble gravel should not be used, since it would leak calcium salts into the water and increase the hardness. To check the gravel a small sample is put into a solution of diluted hydrochloric acid: no gas bubbles should form, otherwise the gravel is not suitable for the aquarium. The sand and gravel mixture should be washed carefully in hot running water in a basin shaken continuously to get rid of the specks of dirt and very fine dust which would muddy the aquarium. To be absolutely certain that all parasitic spores are got rid of it is advisable to leave the gravel in boiling water for about half an hour. In tanks where only aquatic plants are being cultivated a layer of earth can be put under the sand.

The gravel at the bottom of the tank is there not only for esthetic reasons: it serves also as a useful anchorage for aquatic plants which can throw out roots, as a filter, and to trap fish excrement which would otherwise muddy the tank. The gravel bottom should not be flat, but sloped towards a zone where refuse will collect, thus making it easier to remove. The shifting gravel also serves as a hiding-place for certain fish such as loaches which like to bury themselves.

Finally, a collection of small organisms develops among the grains of gravel which feeds on the organic debris and unicellular algae, and which serves as food for many small fish.

In tanks in which fry are being reared or newly acquired fish are under observation it is more practical not to line the bottom of the tank at all.

Lighting

Adequate lighting of an aquarium is essential for the survival of aquatic plants which need luminous energy for their photosynthetic activities and for those fish which need to be able to see the food they are going to eat. Lighting can be natural or artificial.

To obtain sufficient natural lighting the aquarium should be placed near a window so that it gets enough light for 8–10 hours per day. In theory it is not possible to determine how much light is needed as so many factors have to be taken into account. So far as plants are concerned, however, there are those which prosper in a very intense light, while others prefer a weaker light: again, the need for luminous energy varies proportionately

7

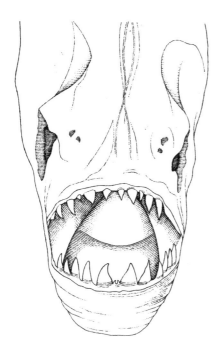

Left: the awesome teeth structure of the Piranha. Opposite: a selection of foods suitable for aquarium fish. From left to right: small crustaceans known as 'water fleas' (*Daphnia*); *Cyclops*, which are even smaller; Tubifex worms.

with the density of the vegetation in the aquarium. So one has to experiment and watch the results. A fairly reasonable indication is given by microscopic algae which cling to and grow on the walls of the tank. If a dark green incrustation, caused by an intense reproduction of green algae, forms within a few days the lighting is excessive; in this case it is a good idea to put the aquarium somewhere less well-lit to avoid the risk (particularly if the tank contains many fish which leave a lot of excrement) of an excessive growth of unicellular green algae which would make the water green and turbid. 'Green water' in itself is not poisonous; like the aquatic plants it develops photosynthetically, but it can easily start to decompose, polluting the water and killing the fish. Also, of course, turbid water prevents the inside of the aquarium from being seen clearly. As soon as there are even slight signs of turbidity the lighting should immediately be reduced and the fish should not be fed for a few days. All excrement and organic refuse – excellent algal fertilisers – should be removed. At the same time the pH should be checked, since too much green algae could result from excessive alkalinity. If necessary the pH should be brought to 6·6–6·8, according to the instructions given in an earlier paragraph. Sometimes where there are few aquatic plants this phenomenon is due to lack of shade. Additional plants will create competition between the plants themselves and the green algae in absorbing luminous energy. As much of the light is retained by the leaves, the growth of the algae is slowed down.

Where the lighting is insufficient a progressive wasting of the aquatic plants can be observed; the new shoots have very little green pigmentation and a brown incrustation forms on the walls inside the tank (brown algae). Natural lighting therefore has difficulties which are both practical and esthetic.

Artificial light on the other hand allows the aquarium to be situated wherever is most convenient. With artificial light the daily output of luminous energy can be controlled by increasing or decreasing the power of the lamp. Ordinary incandescent lamps or fluorescent tubes can be used. The latter have the advantage that they do not give off too much heat, which in the summer could cause an unwanted increase in temperature.

Lighting should be installed at the front of the top of the aquarium. Counter-lighting, although it creates beautiful and sometimes exotic effects, prevents detailed observation of the shapes and colours of the fish.

Generally, aquarium lighting is so constructed that it can be fitted directly on the tank in place of the front part of the cover, but this can be inconvenient, for when the light is extinguished vapour condenses on the inside of the cover with the risk of a short circuit. So instead we suggest that the lighting should be put on top of the glass cover, but not so close that the heat of the lamp causes the cover to crack.

If the tank is in complete darkness care must be taken not to illuminate it suddenly because fish can suffer from any sudden variation of light. If it is not possible to have some artificial light in the late afternoon before the natural light has completely vanished, the light in the room where the aquarium is should be lit first, and then after ten minutes the lighting on the tank. If the aquarium is a large one, big stones will cast shadows and fish which prefer a weaker light can hide there.

Temperature

Temperature is one of the most important factors in the life of the fish which, like all other poikilothermic (cold-blooded) animals such as reptiles and amphibia, assumes the same body temperature as its surroundings. There are eurythermal fish which can live within a wide range of temperature and stenothermal fish which cannot tolerate too much variation from their own optimum temperature. In the aquarium, therefore, the temperature maintained should be suitable for this latter type. It should be made clear that, having stabilised the temperature range according to the types of fish in the aquarium, any variations within that range should always be made very slowly, since sudden changes in temperature lower

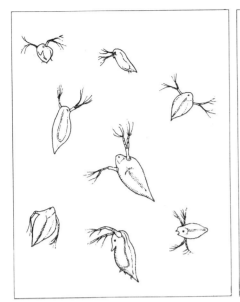  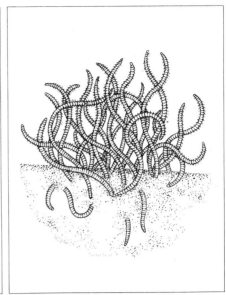

resistance to disease and help to establish epidemics.

Temperature also governs other physical factors, particularly the amount of gas dissolved in the water; a rise in temperature beyond the normal reduces the oxygen content in the aquarium and can cause the death of fish. All other conditions being equal, within certain limits, the lower the temperature the less the possibility of bacterial infection: life is prolonged, the fish increase in size and sexual maturity is retarded.

Optimum temperature varies from fish to fish, but in an aquarium which contains different types of fish compromise is unavoidable: normally a temperature of 24°–25°C is satisfactory for most tropical fish.

An aquarium containing less demanding species can be maintained without independent heating provided that during the winter the tank is placed near a radiator; the lighting used to illuminate the tank can also help maintain the desired temperature. However, the aquarium should be provided with its own heater as soon as practicable – if possible thermostatically controlled so as to maintain a constant water temperature independent of outside conditions. There are various types of heaters with built-in or separate thermostats, of different strengths, suitable for different sizes of aquarium. To avoid breakdown one should check that the part containing the filament is always immersed in the water. The thermometer which measures the temperature of the water should be placed away from the heater where it can be easily seen and will remain in position. If the temperature suddenly rises the thermostat should be checked: very occasionally it can be blocked; a careful cleaning of the silver plugs will avoid this danger.

Oxygenation

Fish breathe by means of their gills, the surfaces of which absorb the oxygen dissolved in the water and expel the carbon dioxide. So the presence of oxygen in the water is of vital importance for the fish. Bearing this in mind, there are certain species which need a high oxygen

pressure and other which can stand considerably lower pressures. Members of the Anabantid family such as *Betta splendens* (plates 53–4) have accessory air-breathing organs above the gills, one at each side; this allows them to breathe a certain amount of atmospheric air, which they do periodically, and they can thus survive in water which contains only a little oxygen. These exceptions apart, the aquarium should be maintained so as to allow a gaseous exchange to take place on the surface of the water, replacing the oxygen which has been consumed, and extracting the carbon dioxide. As already noted earlier, given two tanks of the same volume, the one with the greater surface area should be chosen because it can hold more fish. The glass cover should be raised about five millimetres from the top of the tank to facilitate the exchange of air.

Oxygen consumed by the fish is to some extent renewed photosynthetically by the aquatic plants, which absorb carbon dioxide during the day and give off oxygen. However there should not be too much plant life because at night, when chlorophyllic photosynthesis stops, the aquatic plants lower the pressure of the oxygen and raise that of the carbon dioxide.

In the summer it is particularly important to check that the temperature does not rise beyond what is strictly necessary, because it will lessen the quantity of oxygen which can be dissolved in the water, and at the same time raise the oxygen requirements of the fish because of accelerated metabolic processes, and assist the growth of bacteria and thus the decomposition of organic substances. All these phenomena can lower the oxygen content to a level dangerous for the majority of fish. When the fish remain close to the surface and start to gasp, this is the first sign that the oxygen content of the water has changed.

So as not to run the risk of fish dying from asphyxia, to be able to increase their numbers in an aquarium and to manage to breed those species which need a lot of oxygen, an aerator is needed. One can easily buy a small air compressor (vibrator) which can be connected by

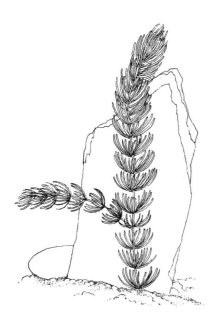

means of a long polythene tube to a special porous stone, which is placed at the bottom of the aquarium. The vibrator should function continuously and the stone then emits a constant stream of myriad small bubbles which rise to the surface, mixing with the water. Still water tends to become stratified, so a continuous stream of gassy bubbles reduces to a minimum the water particles which do not rise to the surface of the tank: the aerator assists the oxygenation of the water principally through the mechanical effect of the air bubbles, which push the lower strata towards the surface where the gas is exchanged. Also there is a gaseous exchange on the surface of the air bubbles themselves, with the oxygen being absorbed into the water and the carbon dioxide turning to gas. It should be pointed out, however, that fish do become dependent on aeration, and this could prove dangerous in an emergency (if the system failed).

The aerator should be connected to special filters which have the triple function of clearing the water, oxygenating it and eliminating toxic gases (see the section on hygiene). The aerator can also usefully be employed to hasten the seasoning of the water for the aquarium, particularly if a special ozoniser is inserted between the pump and the porous stone, since ozone acts as a powerful bactericide.

Aquatic plants

There is no doubt that plants are an important decorative element in an aquarium, but their presence has biological advantages too, which are much more important, if less obvious. They contain chlorophyll which, by means of luminous energy, photosynthetically transforms the carbon dioxide dissolved in the water into organic substances necessary for their growth. During this process oxygen necessary for the fish to breathe is freed. This means that in an aquarium in which plant and animal life are well balanced, the balance of carbon dioxide and oxygen is also maintained. Also, aquatic plants feed on fish excrement. The fish can find a safe hiding place among the aquatic vegetation and live more

quietly in these natural surroundings. Vegetation is almost essential during the breeding season, sometimes because the eggs are attached to the leaves. As we have noted earlier, aquatic plants can prevent the formation of green water. Finally, they also serve as food, both directly for those fish which have a partially vegetarian diet and indirectly for many small organisms, themselves the food of fish.

Artificial plants are also on sale for purely decorative purposes or, in some cases, as an aid to breeding. For reasons explained earlier, however, live plants are always preferable.

There are many different species of aquatic plants on sale and they should be chosen with an eye to their function in the aquarium (decoration, to oxygenate the water, for breeding), bearing in mind that for best results more eggs are laid on those plants with minute leaves (*Myriophyllum, Ceratophyllum, Cabomba,* etc).

Many aquatic plants can be found in lakes and slowly-flowing rivers. If they are collected from these sources they must be carefully washed so as to eliminate all the small snails which are to be found on them, since these could carry parasites. It is essential to isolate these plants in a separate tank for at least a month, rewashing them every ten days, so as to be certain that all parasites have been destroyed or removed.

When it comes to positioning them in the aquarium, a small piece of angler's split lead shot should be attached with special tweezers to those plants which have no roots, and the stems planted in the gravel at the bottom of the tank. Certain aquatic plants (*Elodea, Ceratophyllum*) grow best if they are grouped in clumps.

Often plants which have been collected from lakes or rivers will not tolerate a change of surroundings and lose their leaves after only a short time – even if the lighting is good. This is because of the change of physical and chemical properties of the water (pH, hardness, temperature, etc). The new shoots which form later will adapt well to their surroundings and will develop luxuriantly.

A selection of plants suitable for aquariums. From left to right:
Ceratophyllum demersum, Cabomba caroliniana, Elodea densa.

Feeding

The well-being of the fish also depends on how they are fed. A diet which is too monotonous can quickly cause a lack of some element necessary for growth and the fish will sicken and sometimes die. The secret of efficient feeding therefore is to have a good selection of food, both live and dried.

Another error frequently made is overfeeding. The daily intake of food should be regulated so that it is completely consumed within half an hour of having been administered. Any food which has not been eaten should be removed since it will decompose, muddy the water and create conditions favourable for bacterial growth. It takes only a short time to learn how much food the fish need.

Many aquarists feed back as food, fish which have died in the aquarium, but this brings the risk of spreading a possible infectious or parasitic disease which could have killed the fish in the first place. This practice therefore is to be avoided. Indeed any fish which show signs of physical change should immediately be isolated.

Particular care should be lavished on new arrivals in the aquarium, checking that they always succeed in getting food. Fish of widely differing sizes should not be put together in an aquarium because, with few exceptions, the larger fish will feed on the smaller.

If the aquarium cannot be looked after for prolonged periods of, say, 15–30 days, as can happen during the holidays, feeding becomes difficult. It is not a good idea to entrust this to a novice since he could easily kill all the fish through wrong or over-feeding. If the fish are fed intensively for a week, the plant life increased and the aquarium thoroughly cleaned just before going away, this will be sufficient. Healthy fish will stand a fast like this, making use of their own resources and feeding on those organisms present in the sand at the bottom of the aquarium, or on the leaves of the plants.

Let us now look at the principal foods which are normally used. First, there are dried foods with a high protein content, enriched with vitamins; these can be used as the principal food, alternating those with animal and those with vegetable bases. At least once a week the fish should be fed with pieces of lean meat, liver, chicken or crustacea, raw or cooked; for small fish mixtures of meat and small quantities of egg-yolk are best.

Fish which are predominantly vegetarian can be given greens, fresh or gently boiled, such as lettuce, spinach, courgettes, etc. Living animals should also be included in the diet. In shops selling tropical fish one can buy *Tubifex*, which are long, thin, violet-red aquatic worms (see plate 79). To keep them alive they should be put in a small container with a little water and kept in a cold place or in the refrigerator to reduce their metabolism, and therefore their need of oxygen, to a minimum. If possible it is better to keep them in a container under running water. Before they are fed to the fish, any dead worms should be taken out so as not to pollute the water or poison the fish. It is also possible to buy tubes of freeze-dried *Tubifex* which can be used as a partial substitute for the living kind, the advantage here being that it is easier to store.

Another food rich in energy is the brine shrimp, a small marine crustacean, *Artemia salina*, particularly valuable during the growth period. The caption to plate 77 explains how to breed these organisms from their eggs, which one can now buy.

Hygiene

Even in a well-regulated aquarium it can happen that fish will suddenly die for reasons which are not immediately apparent. In nearly every case the cause is the introduction of some poison into the aquarium due to lack of normal hygienic precautions. The aquarium is an enclosed space rich in organic substances with a temperature of around 25°C and with a high density of living organisms – ideal conditions for the development of infectious and parasitic disease. Any object at all which is to be introduced into the aquarium must be carefully washed in boiling water after having been disinfected – if possible in a solution of water and potassium

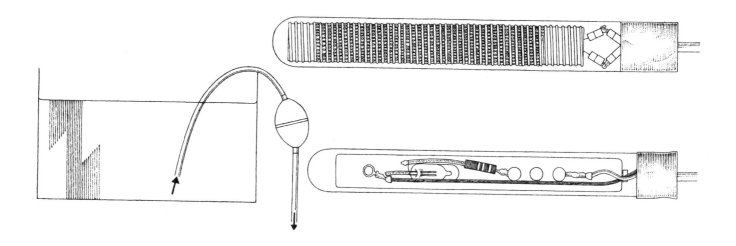

Three pieces of equipment that are virtually essential to the aquarist: siphon (shown in the correct position for use); heater (top); thermostat.

permanganate or formalin (2 or 3 parts per thousand). All apparatus used must be washed every time and stored in clean containers; the hands too must be washed and rinsed well to remove all traces of soap; smokers must not put their cigarette hand into the water, so as to avoid nicotine contamination. It is also advisable to disconnect any electrical apparatus before putting one's hands into the water so as not to run the risk of a bad shock from a faulty earth.

The aquarium should be systematically cleaned at regular intervals, which should be determined by the number of fish. If necessary a siphon can be used: a tube of glass or plastic, the middle part of which broadens into a bulb in which refuse floating in the water can be collected. The sand and gravel at the bottom of the aquarium should be very gently displaced with the siphon and all organic refuse which has accumulated there should be removed. Every time the aquarium is cleaned, the water level has to be readjusted either with soft water (see the paragraph about the properties of water) or with the water collected in the siphon, having removed by decanting or filtering through gauze or cotton any foreign bodies in the bulb. The inside walls of the aquarium can be cleaned with a sponge or, where green algae are encrusted on the sides, with an old safety-razor blade (a special holder can be bought for this purpose). Once or twice a year the aquarium should be thoroughly cleaned; the fish and plants should be transferred to another tank, together with clear water siphoned off from the aquarium, then all the objects from the aquarium (including the gravel from the bottom) should be washed in hot running water. During the cleaning any sudden changes of temperature should be avoided, particularly when water is being added to readjust the level.

If the aquarium is heavily populated and one wishes to space out the cleaning periods with the siphon and yet maintain clear water, an active carbon filter is needed. For small and medium-sized aquariums there are special filters which can be buried in the sand, connected to a small external compressor; in these there is a layer of active carbon which absorbs noxious gases and a layer of perlon which keeps the particles suspended in the water. The intake of water into the filter is caused by the air from the vibrator being forced along the tube, and this also oxygenates the water. For large aquariums of 50 litres or over external filters, also of active carbon, are more efficient. They are worked by small centrifugal pumps which draw in the turbid water, filter it and eject it, clear again, back into the aquarium. This last type of filter is the most efficient and, price apart, can also be used very successfully on smaller aquariums. Every two to six months the filters should be regenerated, the active carbon being replaced and the synthetic fibre being washed with hot running water.

Breeding and rearing fry

Fish can be oviparous, ovoviviparous or viviparous. In ovoviviparous and viviparous species the eggs are retained in the female gonads where the embryos develop, and the female spawns the fry, which are immediately able to swim on their own. Fertilisation is internal: the male has a reproductive organ which is generally formed by the modification of the anal fin (gonopodium) with which the female is fertilised. In oviparous species fertilisation is external: the female spawns the eggs which are then fertilised in the water by a spermatic liquid ejected by the male.

Details of the differing methods of reproduction are given in the captions to the individual photographs; here we are dealing only with the more general characteristics. In ovoviviparous and viviparous fish, a certain time after mating (the length varies according to the individual species) the female is isolated in a container with plenty of food and vegetation to allow the fry to escape and hide, since they could be devoured by their mother. Breeding cages are much more practical for this purpose: they are small containers with slits at the bottom into which the females are put, and are placed in a larger receptacle containing 1½–2 litres of water. The fry can escape into the larger receptacle through the slits in the bottom (see sketch on page 7).

For the reproduction of oviparous fish, the pair should be isolated in a tank with thick natural or artificial vegetation and, except in those cases where the parent fish should look after the eggs and the fry in the first stage of development, it is always a good idea to remove the parent fish as soon as the eggs have been spawned, so that they do not eat them.

A difficult problem is the feeding of new-born fry and this varies according to their size. Fry spawned by viviparous and ovoviviparous fish are generally a few millimetres in length and they can immediately be fed with dry pulverised food, alternating with homogenised foods and the larvae of the brine shrimp (see caption to plate 77).

The fry of oviparous fish on the other hand are much smaller and in their first state of development need live food consisting of microscopic organisms. To have these available in quantity one puts some hay to soak in water at a temperature of 25°–30°C, adding green water or water siphoned off from the bottom of the aquarium, and later some decomposing lettuce leaves. After a few days if a specimen of this is examined under the microscope a mass of small unicellular organisms including such creatures as *Amoeba*, *Paramecium* and *Vorticella* can be seen. These are known as infusoria, which are excellent nourishment for these very small fry. To keep this culture of infusoria alive for several days, water in which greens have been boiled should be added to the mixture. To give an even more balanced diet for these fry small quantities of egg-yolk can be stirred into the water. To accelerate their growth, the aquarium can be lit throughout the day and night.

Preventing disease

Diseases which can attack fish are very numerous and diagnosis difficult, being generally possible only for specialists. So it is our purpose in this brief account to note the general precautions for preventing disease rather than to indicate diagnoses and cures.

Sharp variations of temperature reduce the resistance of the fish to infection and favour the growth of certain latent parasites such as 'white-spot' disease (*Ichthyophthirius*). Overcrowding also produces a general lowering of vitality.

Almost all infections and infestations which occur are due to lack of normal precautions and hygiene. Before being put into the aquarium, and as soon as new fish are acquired, they should be isolated 'in quarantine' for at least 20–30 days. They should be fed a varied diet, preferably live food, and carefully observed to assess the state of their health. Only if they feed voluntarily, have no difficulty in swimming, their colours stay bright, the fins are perfect and no patches appear on their skins, can the newly acquired fish be put into the aquarium; it is unlikely that they will be carrying infectious disease. But the fish in the aquarium must be checked systematically and any which show signs of discomfort should be isolated immediately.

A disease which occurs frequently in aquariums as a result of a sudden lowering of the temperature is 'white-spot' disease, caused by a skin protozoon, *Ichthyophthirius multifiliis*: all parts of the body, including gills and fins of fish affected by this disease are covered in small white spots. To cure it, the water temperature should be maintained at 30°C for several days; the addition of chloromycetin in the ratio 200 milligrammes : 10 litres of water is even more efficacious.

The skin fluke (*Gyrodactylus elegans*) is a small worm (trematode) parasite of the skin, provided with a sucker with which it attaches itself to the epidermis of the fish. They are not visible to the naked eye and it needs a strong magnifying glass to be able to identify them. Fish infected with these worms are easily recognisable: they have difficulty in swimming because of the weight of the worms attached to their bodies. To disinfect the aquarium, introduce 1 ml of fresh formalin for every 10 litres of water while aerating it strongly, repeating the

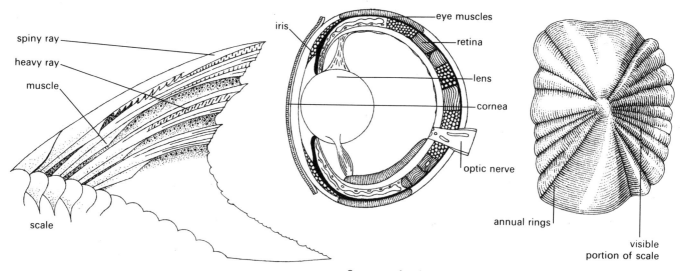

Structure of various parts of a typical fish. Far left: fin rays of the Tinfoil Barb (*Barbus schwanenfeldi*). Centre: cross-section of the eye. Right: fish scale (x3).

dose after 3–4 days. After a week it is advisable to give the aquarium a general clean and change the water.

Weak fish or those with excoriations of the skin risk being attacked by a fungus (*Saprolegnia*) which manifests itself as white or grey cotton-like tufts on the epidermis of the affected fish. If it is not too extensive it can be treated successfully by 30 seconds in a solution of water and Malachite Green. Generally, however, it is better to destroy the affected fish rather than run the risk of the disease spreading.

Marine aquariums

The aquarist who has successfully bred and reared fresh-water fish can try his hand at rearing salt-water fish; these present greater difficulties, although with modern methods and equipment marine tanks are becoming very popular and increasingly easy to keep. The improvements in filters with bases of special resins and the possibility of preparing artificial sea water have simplified the problems. In the final photographs in the book one can admire the bizarre shapes and splendid colours of some of these tropical salt-water fish; this may inspire the enthusiast to venture into a new field.

Metric Equivalents

1 litre	= 0·220 British (imperial) gallon
	= 0·264 US gallon
1 millilitre (ml)	= 0·035 fluid ounces (British)
	= 0·034 fluid ounces (US)
1 metre	= 3 feet 3·4 inches
1 centimetre (cm)	= 0·394 inches
1 millimetre (mm)	= 0·039 inches
1 gram	= 0·035 ounces (avoirdupois)
1 milligram	= 0·015 grains

Water Temperature

Conversion °C to °F

$$°C = (°F - 32)/1·8 \qquad °F = 32 + (°C \times 1·8)$$

Temp. °C	Temp. °F
0	32·0
10	50·0
11	51·8
12	53·6
13	55·4
14	57·2
15	59·0
16	60·8
17	62·6
18	64·4
19	66·2
20	68·0
21	69·8
22	71·6
23	73·4
24	75·2
25	77·0
26	78·8
27	80·6
28	82·2
29	84·2
30	86·0
31	87·8
32	89·6
33	91·4
34	93·2
35	95·0

Index to aquarium fishes illustrated

Acanthophthalmus kuhlii sumatranus 29
Actinia, see *Calliactis parasitica*
Aequidens curviceps 67
Ambassis lala, see *Chanda ranga*
American Flag Fish, see *Jordanella floridae*
Amphiprion percula 85
Angel Fish, see *Pterophyllum eimekei*
Aphyosemion calliurum ahli 39
Argus Scat, see *Scatophagus argus*
Artemia salina 77
Astronotus ocellatus 73
Balistapus undulatus 83
Barb, see *Barbus nigrofasciatus*
Barbus nigrofasciatus 19
Barbus schwanenfeldi 25
Barbus tetrazona 22–3
Barbus titteya 24
Betta splendens (cover) 53–4
Black Molly, see *Mollienesia latipinna*
Botia Macracanthus 28
Brachydanio rerio 16
Brachygobius xanthozona 76
Butterfly Fish, see *Chaetodon sp.*
Calliactis parasitica 81
Cardinal Tetra, see *Cheirodon axelrodi*
Carassius auratus 17, 20–1
Chaetodon sp. 89
Chanda ranga 61
Cheirodon axelrodi 9–10
Chelmon rostratus 87
Cherry Barb, see *Barbus titteya*
Cichlasoma festivum 72
Cichlasoma meeki 71
Clown Fish, see *Amphiprion percula*
Clown Loach, see *Botia macracanthus*
Cobitis taenia 30–1
Cobitis taenia bilineata 30–1
Cobitis taenia puta 30–1
Coffer Fish, see *Ostracion sp.*
Colisa lalia 52
Corydoras sp. 32–3
Crossbow Fish, see *Balistapus undulatus*
Cuprina, see *Pomacea bridgesi diffusa*

Dermogenys pusillus 36
Dwarf Gourami, see *Colisa lalia*
Epiplatys dageti 38
Feather Fish, see *Gymnocorymbus ternetzi*
Firemouth, see *Cichlasoma meeki*
Gambusia affinis, see *Lebistes reticulatus*
Gasteropelecus sternicla 3
Ghost Glass Catfish, see *Kryptopterus bicirrhis*
Glass Catfish, see *Kryptopterus bicirrhis*
Glass Fish, see *Chanda ranga*
Gorgonzola Fish, see *Trichogaster trichopterus*
Gymnocorymbus ternetzi 2
Gyrinocheilus aymonieri 26–7
Harlequin Fish, see *Rasbora hetermorpha*
Hatchet Fish, see *Gasteropelecus sternicla*
Helostoma temmincki 57
Hemichromis bimaculatus 74
Hemigrammus pulcher 7
Heniochus acuminatus 82
Hermit Crab 81
Hyphessobrycon callistus 4
Hyphessobrycon innesi 6
Hyphessobrycon pulchripinnis 5
Jordanella floridae 37
Kissing Gourami, see *Helostoma temmincki*
Kryptopterus bicirrhis 34
Labeo bicolor 18
Labeotropheus trewavasae 66
Lace-Tail, see *Lebistes reticulatus*
Macropodus opercularis 55–6
Marbled Cichlid, see *Astronotus ocellatus*
Mesogonistius chaetodon 60
Millions Fish, see *Lebistes reticulatus*
Moenkhausia sanctae filomenae 8
Monodactylus argenteus 62
Nauplius, see *Artemia salina*
Neon Tetra, see *Hyphessobrycon innesi*
Notopterus chitala 1
Ostracion sp. 86
Paradise Fish, see *Macropodus opercularis*
Pelmatochromis kribensis 75
Penguin Fish, see *Thayeria sp.*
Petticoat Tetra, see *Gymnocorymbus ternetzi*

Platy, see *Xiphophorus maculatus*
Platypoecilus maculatus, see *Xiphophorus maculatus*
Poecilia latipinna 44–5
Poecilia reticulatus 40–3
Pomacanthus sp. 84
Pomacanthus imperator, see *Pomacanthus sp.*
Pomacea bridgesi diffusa 78
Pseudemys scripta elegans 79–80
Pseudemys scripta troostii 79–80
Pseudotropheus auratus 65
Pterophyllum eimekei 68–70
Pterophyllum scalare 68–70
Puffer, see *Tetraodon fluviatilis*
Rainbow Fish, see *Lebistes reticulatus*
Rasbora heteromorpha 14
Red Breasted Piranha, see *Serrasalmus (Rooseveltiella) nattereri*
Scalare, see *Pterophyllum scalare*
Scatophagus argus 63
Scatophagus argus (var. rubrifrons) 64
Serrasalmus sp. 12–13
Serrasalmus (Rooseveltiella) nattereri 12–13
Sucking Catfish, see *Gyrinocheilus aymonieri*
Sumatra Barb, see *Barbus tetrazona*
Swordtail, see *Xiphophorus helleri*
Synodontis migriventris 35
Tanichthys albonubes 15
Telescope Fish, see *Carassius auratus*
Tetraodon fluviatilis 58
Tetraodon palembangensis 59
Thalassoma lunare 88
Thayeria sp. 11
Tiger Barb, see *Barbus tetrazona*
Trichogaster trichopterus 51
Trigger Fish, see *Balistapus undulatus*
Turtles, see *Pseudemys scripta troostii*
Upside-down Catfish, see *Synodontis nigriventris*
Wagtail Platy, see *Xiphophorus maculatus*
Wasp Fish, see *Brachygobius Xanthozona*
Weeping Fish, see *Carassius auratus*
Xiphophorus helleri 46–7
Xiphophorus maculatus 48–50
Zebra Fish, see *Brachydanio rerio*

1

1 Feather Fish or Knife Fish, *Notopterus chitala* (Hamilton-Buchanan). This species is found in the inland waterways of Thailand and the islands of the Malay Archipelago. Its shape is elongated, very flat, and there is a fin running along the underside of the body, merging to form both anal and caudal fin. This single fin, which undulates continuously, allows the fish to move quickly both forwards and backwards without any lateral body movement. It breathes not only through its gills but also by means of a natatory vescicle (swim-bladder) modified into a respiratory organ. Consequently it will rise frequently to the surface to breathe. Only the fry of this species can be kept in an aquarium (in their adult state they grow to half a metre): They prefer the darkness and therefore need a hiding-place during the day. At night they are very active and hunt for food. The water temperature should be maintained at 25°–28°C.

2

3

2 Black Widow, *Gymnocorymbus ternetzi*
(Boulenger). Lives in Brazil (Mato Grosso, in the
basins of the Paraguay, the Guaporé and the
Negro). Its common name is Black Widow because
of its markings, but the black fades to grey as the
fish matures. It is also known as a Petticoat Tetra
because of its appearance: it has a large anal fin
which extends from the latter half of the body to
the caudal stem, giving the impression of a
petticoat. It is sometimes possible to distinguish the
male from the female during the breeding season,
when the female's belly is swollen with eggs and
there are white marks on the caudal fin of the male.
This species adapts well at 25°–30°C and
reproduction is fairly simple: the ripe females are
isolated in a container and fed for several days with
plenty of live food (small insects, *Tubifex*, *Artemia
salina*, etc). An aquarium with plenty of plant life
is prepared into which a male and a female are put,
and the fertilised eggs are deposited on the leaves of
the plants.

3 Hatchet Fish, *Gasteropelecus sternicla*
(Linnaeus). Found in the Amazon and its
tributaries. This fish, which can grow to 5 or 6 cm,
is known as a Hatchet Fish since it so clearly
resembles a hatchet. It is a species which easily
adapts to aquarium life if the water temperature is
maintained at between 25° and 30°C.

4 Blood Characin, *Hyphessobrycon callistus*
(Boulenger). Distributed in Guyana, Central
Amazonia and the River Paraguay. In an aquarium
it will grow to a size of 3–4 cm and at 22°–28°C is
capable of reproduction.

5 Lemon Tetra, *Hyphessobrycon pulchripinnis*
(Ahl). Very good for tropical aquariums. Its needs
are those of the preceding species. To get a pair to
breed one has only to raise the water temperature
to 28°C and add some plants to the aquarium.

6 Neon Tetra, *Hyphessobrycon innesi* (Myers). Found in the Peruvian region of the Amazon, it requires a water temperature of 22°–24°C. Although it was once very expensive, it now sells at a price within the reach of most aquarists. It is a fish which enlivens an aquarium with its gaudy colouring. The back part and underside of the body are bright red while the upper part is greeny grey. There is a streak of brilliant blue from the rim of the eye to the edge of the caudal stem which gives a remarkable iridescence, and it is for this reason that it is commonly known as the Neon Tetra. If there are a lot of these fish in the same aquarium a most beautiful effect is created by many luminous points moving through the water. Because of the small size of the fish which are normally offered for sale (1½–2 cm, maximum length 4 cm) they should not be put in an aquarium containing fish with aggressive instincts. Breeding these interesting fish presents certain problems. All the apparatus should be thoroughly cleaned – sterilised if possible. Successful spawning depends upon the quality of the water, which should be very soft (from a spring or distilled water mixed with a little drinking water) and slightly acid (about pH 6); the mating pair also need some aquatic plants – *Myrophyllum* or *Fontinalis*. The male fish is identifiable by its graceful outline while the female should be large with a well dilated belly. The pair should be at least one year old (2–3 cm in length). It is advisable to have a large aquarium with a water level of 10–15 cm and water which has been left to season for 15–20 days.

6

7

7 Beacon or Head-and-tail-light Fish, *Hemigrammus pulcher* (Ladiges). Like the Neon Tetra, this fish comes from the Peruvian region of the Amazon. It grows to a length of 6 cm; it does not disturb and is not disturbed by other species which are present in the same tank. Its colouring seems to vary with the angle of incidence of the light: the dominant is a silver yellow tending towards brown on the back while below the caudal stem it is bright blue black; there are patches of orange red on the caudal stem (unfortunately not visible) in this photograph because of the lighting) and above the eye.

8 Red-eye Tetra, *Moenkhausia sanctae-filomenae* (Steindachner). This fish is widely found in the Paraguay and Paranaiba rivers. It is suitable for aquariums with a temperature of 22°–28°C in which it will grow to a maximum length of 6–7 cm. The swollen belly of the female is the only distinguishing feature between the sexes. The edges of the scales are picked out in black, which gives a rhombic design on a dominant silvery-grey colour. The upper half of the eye is a brilliant red and the caudal stem is circled with two rings, yellow and black.

9 Cardinal Tetra, *Cheirodon axelrodi* (Schultz). Found in the Rio Negro and in the small forest pools of this region, where it grows to approximately 4 cm. It is known as Cardinal Tetra because of the colour of the underside of its body: a beautiful cardinal red. Its habits, method of reproduction and dimorphism are very similar to those of the Neon Tetra, from which it is easily distinguished because the red colouring extends along the whole of the underside, below the iridiscent blue streak.

8

9

10 Many aquarists prefer to keep several small aquariums as well as one large one; in each tank fish of the same or very similar species are kept, which form shoals of identical fish and create a very pleasing effect, as can be seen from this photograph of young Cardinal Tetras.

11 Penguin Fish, *Thayeria sp.* (Eigenmann). These fish are found in the Amazon basin and will breed when they reach their full size of around 6 cm (maximum length 8 cm). Their resemblance to the penguin is due to the longitudinal black stripe which runs the length of the body and down to the under lobe of the caudal stem. It often assumes a characteristic position when it is not swimming, floating at an angle with its head much higher than its tail. This fish adapts very easily to life in an aquarium maintained at a temperature of 22°–28°C. It is advisable to buy fry because mature fish have sharp teeth and are liable to attack small non-aggressive fish and devour them. Adult fish can be isolated for reproduction, bearing in mind that the female can be recognised only by her swollen belly.

10

11

12

13

12-13 Piranha, *Serrasalmus sp*. (Lacapède). Fish of this species are widely found, particularly in the basins of the Amazon, Parana and the Plata. They can grow to as much as 25–30 cm. Their colouring varies according to age and surroundings and thus they are not always easily recognised. The fish pictured here is probably a young *Serrasalmus (Rooseveltiella) nattereri* (Kner), commonly known as a Red-breasted Piranha because of the colouring of its belly, throat and anal fin which gets more pronounced as it gets older. Generally a black spot forms behind the gill cover. In an aquarium these fish should be kept at a temperature of 23°–29°C and completely isolated from fish of other species. Care must also be taken when transferring them from one tank to another because they can bite viciously. To give some idea of its savagery: if a herd of animals fords a river in which there are piranhas some of the beasts may be completely devoured, and in a very short time only the bones, picked clean, are left. It will also attack humans, particularly if they are wounded, because blood excites it and makes it even more voracious. In the picture on the right its extraordinarily strong and sharp teeth can be seen. In regions where these fish are particularly common there are warning stations to give the alarm immediately any approaching shoals are sighted. It is because of these bloodthirsty qualities, rare in such a small fish, that the piranha is so widely sold. In captivity, however, if no live animals are available this species can be fed on dead fish.

14
15

14 Harlequin Rasbora, *Rasbora heteromorpha* (Duncher). An Asiatic species, found in Malacca, Sumatra and Thailand. It is known as the Harlequin Rasbora because of its bright colouring: a black triangle covers the back half of the body, tapering to a point at the end of the caudal stem. Their maximum length is 5 cm and they are very much prized by aquarists for their lively yet gentle temperament. They need a water temperature of 22°–28°C. In their countries of origin they are so widely found that they are often used as fertiliser. They like to live in shoals and it is advisable therefore to keep many in the same aquarium.

15 White Cloud Mountain Minnow, *Tanichthys albonubes* (Linnaeus). This fish, a native of China (Canton), lives in cool temperatures (10°–28°C) and spawns readily. The ripe female should be put with the male at a temperature of 22°–24°C and the mating pair should be fed on *Artemia salina* to prevent them from eating the eggs.

16 Zebra Fish, *Brachydanio rerio* (Hamilton-Buchanan). This fish is found in Eastern India, particularly in the Ganges. When it is fully grown this little fish is only 4–5 cm. It is commonly known as a Zebra Fish or Zebra Danio because of the horizontal stripes which run the length of its body. It is not particularly concerned about temperature (21°–30°C) but the best temperature for spawning is 24°C. The parent fish (2–3 males and 1 ripe female) should be well fed and placed in an aquarium provided with plenty of natural or artificial vegetation; if not, the eggs are liable to be eaten by the parent fish.

17 Goldfish, *Carassius auratus* (Linnaeus). Originating in the temperate regions of Asia, this fish has been introduced into all parts of the world. It will live in temperatures varying from 5°–25°C.

16

17

18

19

18 Red-tailed Black Shark, *Labeo bicolor* (Smith). This fish is widely found in fresh-running water in Thailand. It can grow to a fairly large size (maximum length 12 cm). The whole of its body, including the dorsal, anal and ventral fins, is a pleasing shade of velvety black in sharp contrast to the orange red of the caudal fins. The dorsal fin is large and flag-like. It adapts to aquariums with temperatures of 23°–28°C and it will not harm other fish; however, it needs some shelter, such as a rock, so as to hide from bright light. It feeds on refuse and organisms which it finds among the gravel at the bottom of the tank.

19 Nigger Barb, Black Ruby, *Barbus nigrofasciatus* (Günther). This fish is caught in the deep and slow-running waters of Ceylon. It has a maximum length of 6 cm and tolerates a temperature of 23°–27°C. It brings an aquarium to life because it is very active, but this means that it needs plenty of space. It is easily distinguished from other similar barbs by three or four blackish, uneven transverse bands. The male is redder than the female (particularly during the breeding season). Its method of reproduction is typical of its type.

20-1 Goldfish, *Carassius auratus* (linnaeus). This species varies enormously in its colour, shape, length, and number of fins. These variations are frequently due to mutation and are thus hereditary. Such fish are curiosities in an aquarium, where they can live for decades. However one must ensure that they can get at the food: due to bodily modifications they are very slow-moving and faster fish can take the food from them. The two specimens photographed exhibit clear differences in the level of their eyes. The fish in plate 20 is known as a Weeping Fish; the other (plate 21) has very protuberant eyes which have earned it the name of Telescope Fish.

22
23

24

22-3 Tiger Barb, Sumatra Barb, *Barbus tetrazona* (Bleeker). Comes from Sumatra and Borneo which gives it the name by which it is commonly known, Sumatra Barb, although the name which suits it better is Tiger Barb. It is one of the most beautiful of the barbs: on a silvery body with rose-coloured hues are four transverse bands of rather beautiful black, one of which passes through the eye. This fish is very hardy if kept at a temperature of 22°–32°C. In an aquarium, individual fish of this species tend to form shoals and to swim with synchronised movements. Adult fish of this type can reach a maximum length of 7 cm and are apt to molest fish with large fins, which they are inclined to nip – apparently in fun. They breed easily: a male (which has a red mouth when in a breeding condition) and a ripe female should be put, during the evening, into a tank with plenty of aquatic plants. Generally the female spawns next morning as soon as it starts to get light.

24 Cherry Barb, *Barbus titteva* (Deraniyagala). Named Cherry Barb on account of its red colouring (particularly noticeable in the male when in a breeding condition) this fish comes from Ceylon. It is a species which, like other barbs, breeds easily, but the fry are very small and find it difficult to feed.

25 Tinfoil Barb, *Barbus schwanenfeldi* (Bleeker). Found in the Malayan Peninsula, Thailand, Sumatra and Borneo where it grows rapidly, reaching a length of 30 cm or more.

25

26
27

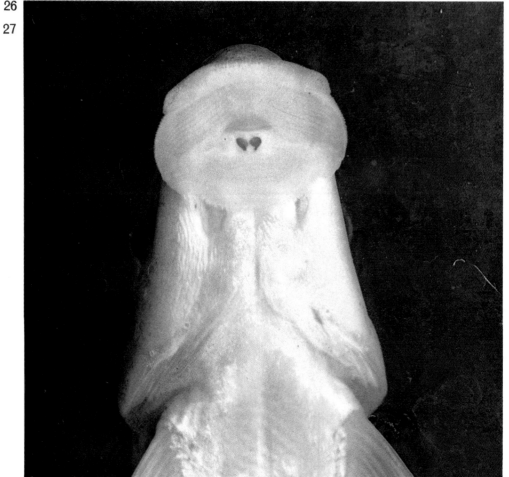

26-7 Sucker Loach, *Gyrinocheilus aymonieri* (Tirant). Widely found in the fresh waters of Thailand, it is very interesting in an aquarium because of its special characteristic: a sucking organ which is very developed and surrounds the ventral mouth. With this sucker the fish can adhere to flat surfaces and scrape off the algae on which it feeds. So it is a useful helper in an aquarium as it eliminates the filter of green and brown algae which invariably forms on tank walls, rocks and the leaves of aquatic plants; its diet needs to be augmented, however, with vegetarian food. This assiduous scavenger cannot take in water to oxygenate its gills as other fish do, and it has an auxiliary gill above the gill covers for this purpose. In aquariums it is advisable to keep only young fish of this species because the adult fish (15–25 cm in length) are very quarrelsome and aggressive.

28 Clown Loach, *Botia macracanthus* (Bleeker).
Found in Sumatra and Borneo and can grow to a
length of 25 cm. In household aquariums, therefore,
it is best to keep only the smaller specimens. It is a
fish with a very pleasing and brilliant colouring. The
slender body is an orange red with three wide very
black bands, the first covering the eye completely.
It is very active at night and during the day it tends
to hide among the plants or behind rocks and will
often dig itself a lair in the sand. It tolerates a
temperature of between 23°–28°C.

29 Coolie Loach, *Acanthophthalmus kuhlii
sumatranus* (Fraser-Brunner). This sub-species is
found in Sumatra. It is eel-like in both its shape and
its movements. Running along the length of its
body are incompletely formed brown transverse
bands, one of which passes through the eye. Its
basic colour is orange yellow, brilliant on the male,
less so on the female. This fish scavenges the bottom
of the tank, that is, it lives on food discarded by
other fish and spends its day searching through the
sand with its sensory barbels, feeding freely on the
various small organisms buried there.

28

29

30-1 Spined Loach, *Cobitis taenia* (Linnaeus).
This species, which is commonly found in rivers and
lakes, is widely diffused throughout Europe and
Asia. It lives naturally at temperatures between 5°
and 25°C, but in an aquarium the ideal temperature
is between 16° and 20°C. At the base of each of its
pectoral fins the male has a lens-shaped formation
(known as Canestrini's palette); it is much smaller
than the female (a maximum length of 7–8 cm as
compared with her 12–13 cm). During the
reproductive period the ripe female looks less
slender than the male. In this species the
phenomenon of sex reversal can be observed: once
the male has reached a certain age it undergoes
bodily changes and becomes female; in the
transitional period from one sex to another the fish
has vestigial elements of both sexes in its gonads.
The shape of the body varies enormously and at
one time those fish which had a long horizontal
band (plate 30) were classed as belonging to the
sub-species *Cobitis taenia bilineata,* and those
with a lot of large round spots to *Cobitis taenia
puta.* However, experimental treatment with
hormones has indicated that the same fish can in
fact show both types of markings at different
periods of its life. They can reproduce in spring
provided that there is plenty of sand and mud in
which the mating pair can deposit the eggs.

32-3 Catfish, *Corydoras sp.* (Lacepède). This
species is very common in South America,
particularly in the Amazon basin. The fish easily
adapts to tropical aquariums and is one of the best
scavengers. The ventral mouth is surrounded by
barbels (plate 33) and the fish is almost incessantly
on the move, feeding on matter discarded by other
fish.

34 Glass Catfish, *Kryptopterus bicirrhis* (Cuvier and Valenciennes). This fish is imported from Indonesia (Borneo, Java, Sumatra). It is much sought by aquarists, and is known as the Glass Catfish (or Ghost Glass Catfish) because it is extremely transparent: the skeleton and internal organs are clearly visible; if lit by direct light it becomes iridescent. It has a very slim body and an anal fin which runs the length of the underbelly but which is not attached to the two-forked caudal stem. By contrast, the dorsal fin is extremely small, almost a bone. It has two maxillary barbels on either side of its mouth. Its habits are singular: it will remain in an oblique position without moving for hours on end, without any support and moving only the anal fin. It is a long fish (maximum length 10–15 cm). It is completely inoffensive but adapts initially with difficulty as it is timid and easily frightened. It is not suitable for an aquarium which contains very lively fish, preferring to live in shoals with its own kind and with plenty of room and lots of vegetation, the temperature between 20°–25°C. At the time of writing it has not yet been bred in captivity, and no noticeable sexual difference is known.

35 Upside-down Catfish, *Synodontis nigriventris* (David). This fish comes from Africa (the Congo basin). It is a peaceful, rather small fish, and lives on vegetarian food. Its body has irregular spots of dark chestnut which often fuse to form transverse bands. It differs from most other fish in that its belly is darker than the rest of its body – indeed the underbelly is completely black, hence its name *nigriventris*. This black underbelly is a form of camouflage as it normally swims belly upwards, a curious habit which has given it its common name.

36   Half-beak, *Dermogenys pusillus* (von Hasselt).
These fish are widely found in the fresh and
brackish waters of Borneo, Java, Sumatra,
Malacca and Thailand. It will tolerate an aquarium
temperature of 20°–25°C so long as it has plenty of
space. It swims on the surface of the water and
sometimes there is a danger of its colliding with the
wall of the aquarium as it cannot see the
transparent glass. It has a spindle-shaped body and
a beak-shaped mouth. In Thailand it is selectively
bred for its aggressive qualities: two males will
fight, hurling themselves at each other and gripping
and immobilising the adversary with strong
maxillaries. The difference between the fighting of
this species and that of the Siamese Fighting Fish
(*Betta splendens*) is that here the fight is bloodless
and only rarely does one of the combatants die,
although it can happen that the pointed tip of one
accidentally penetrates the gill of the other, causing
a hemorrhage. Specially bred specimens will fight
for hours, while those in their natural state retire
after 10–20 minutes. At a certain point the weaker
will no longer react to the attacks of the stronger,
and the fight is abandoned. Reproduction: the
male, with a reproductive organ formed from a
modified anal fin, fertilises the female, who after
about two months spawns fry which are
immediately able to swim. The fish is difficult to
breed and will present a challenge to the ambitious
aquarist. To raise a brood can be considered no
mean achievement.

37   American Flag Fish, *Jordanella floridae*
(Goode and Beane). This species is found in the
United States (Florida) and is in great demand for
its brilliant colouring which is reminiscent of the
American flag. It needs a lot of space and an
abundant supply of algae, as it is vegetarian; it
requires a temperature of 20°–25°C. The male is
more strongly coloured than the female.

38 Red-chinned Panchax, *Epiplatys dageti* (Sauvage). Found throughout Africa (from Sierra Leone to Ghana). The name *Epiplatys* refers to the fact that its upper profile is almost rectilinear, a useful attribute as it normally lives near the surface. Although it is small (maximum length 6 cm) this fish is very similar in its appearance and feeding habits to the pike: it is a voracious hunter which swallows any fish it can, so it should obviously not be kept in an aquarium containing small fish. It requires a temperature of 20°–30°C. Its rectilinear olive-green body has 5–6 black, broken, transverse bands, and the male is more brilliantly coloured than the female: its back is stippled with small red spots and the lower maxillary is bright red (hence its alternative name of Fire-mouth). In an aquarium with well-seasoned water and plenty of floating plants, reproduction is quite easy; indeed two or more mating pairs can be put together at the same time. The female lays each egg separately and it is immediately fertilised by the male – in all a total of 15–20 eggs a day. This can happen one day a week for several weeks. The eggs are attached to the plants and hatch after 10–20 days. After all the eggs have been deposited it is a good idea to isolate those plants which have eggs attached.

39 Lyretail, *Aphyosemion calliurum* ahli (Myers). This species is found in the tropical regions of West Africa. It is a very elegant fish, particularly the male, for it is finely and brilliantly marked with different colours: the underside of the male tends to be blue, that of the female red. Several females can live together in an aquarium at a temperature of 22°–26°C, but males cannot be put together because they tend to tear each other's fins. A small receptacle containing plants with very small leaves and plenty of food gives ideal conditions for the eggs of a mating pair to be deposited.

4

40-3 Guppy, *Poecilia reticulatus* (Peters). Comes from Barbados, Trinidad, Venezuela, Guyana and northern Brazil. This is without doubt the most popular of all tropical fish. Guppies feed on small crustaceans and insects, and for this reason they have been introduced into mosquito-affected regions as a biological check on the aquatic larvae of these insects. For this same purpose a very similar fish (*Gambusia affinis*), which can tolerate much lower temperatures and even survive in winter, has been introduced into colder climates. Guppies are particularly well adapted for aquarium life: they are strong and without any particular temperature needs (17°–30°C). Male and female are very easily distinguished because they are very differently marked. The female (maximum length 6 cm) has a round belly and for most of the time has no coloured marking except for two large black abdominal spots. The male (plates 42–3) is smaller (up to 3 cm) and more slender with long fins. Its patterned body and fins have given it the name of Rainbow Veiltail Guppy. It is not necessary to isolate the breeding pair from other fish, since the male courts the female incessantly with curious movements until he succeeds in impregnating her with his gonopodium (modified anal fin). These fish are ovoviviparous, so the eggs are not laid but retained within the female gonads. About 25 days after impregnation the female becomes enormously swollen and should be isolated in a tank with plenty of vegetation and food, to reduce the danger of her eating the fry. After a further 5–10 days the female spawns 30–60 small guppies which immediately take flight, pursued by their mother. An interesting phenomenon is that every 30–40 days for several months after the first spawning the female spawns a new generation of fry without being impregnated again. It has been ascertained that after the first impregnation the female retains sperm for many months, using it as necessary for her monthly cycle of reproduction. The fry grow quickly and after three months they are sexually mature, but to maintain a healthy strain, mating should only be allowed after six months. The many different varieties which can be found are not haphazard but have hereditary characteristics. Through long selective procedures, breeders have isolated many strains with characteristics which are found in successive generations: Red Veiltail Guppy, *Poecilia reticulatus* (plates 42–3), in which the tail fin is exceptionally long and generous is an example of this. Mutants with organic and structural anomalies have also been obtained: in aquariums treated with formalin, a chemical agent with a mutagenic effect, new strains of guppies have appeared with a very short vertebral column (plates 40–1, male and female respectively).

44-5 Sailfin Black Molly, *Poecilia latipinna* (Le Sueur). This species is found from South Carolina to Yucatan in Mexico. The two fish shown here are of a specially bred strain, completely black, commonly known as Black Molly. They are lively fish, suitable for aquariums with a temperature of 20°–25°C with plenty of vegetation, on which they feed, and with slightly salty water obtained by adding 3–4 teaspoons of kitchen salt to every 10 litres of water (this degree of salinity does not harm the other fish). Their method of reproduction is similar to that of guppies. The photographs show clearly the difference between the two sexes in this ovoviviparous species. In plate 44 the male's tubular-shaped gonopodium, formed by the modified anal fin, can be seen; in plate 45 the female's anal fin is complete, slightly drawn back compared with the two ventral fins. Unfortunately, in the strains which are bred in small aquariums the beautiful fin is very much smaller. A recent change in nomenclature for Mollies from *Mollienisia* to *Poecilia* is generally accepted.

46

47

46-7 Swordtail, *Xiphophorus helleri* (Heckel). This popular aquarium fish is found in many rivers in Guatemala and southern Mexico and in its natural state it can reach a maximum of 12–13 cm. In an aquarium it is much smaller. It has no special dietary needs and quickly accustoms itself to dried foods; it needs a temperature of 21°–25°C. There are many different variations of colouring but a typical example is greeny yellow with a longitudinal red stripe running the length of its body. The green variety, which has yellow and red horizontal stripes neatly dividing an almost uniformly green body, is very beautiful. The method of reproduction is similar to that described for guppies, and with an issue of 30–100 fry. The female should be removed as quickly as possible after spawning since she is apt to eat all the fry. The female (plate 46, bottom) is much larger than the male and more thickset, with a swollen belly protected from the light by two black spots. The male (plate 46 above) has a slender body and its fin-like reproductive organ is where the anal fin is on the female. A long pointed 'sword' runs from the lower part of the caudal fin; hence its name Swordtail, although this originally referred to the stiletto-shaped reproductive organ. The aquarist who breeds these fish will be able to witness the phenomenon of sex reversal. Often, after many reproductive cycles the adult female begins to undergo bodily changes: the anal fin is transformed into a gonopodium and the bottom half of the caudal fin lengthens into a 'sword' until the fish becomes a fertile male. Plate 47 shows a female which has changed sex; it is larger than the normal male (right).

50

48-50 Platy, *Xiphophorus maculatus* (Günther). Like the previous species, this one is found in Guatemala and Mexico. However it is smaller (plate 49), adult males reaching about 4 cm and females about 7 cm in length. They are mature when they are 2–3 cm. In an aquarium they grow to a smaller size and adapt themselves perfectly if the temperature is between 21°–25°C, 2–3 teaspoons of kitchen salt are added to every 10 litres of water, and a little tender salad added to their normal diet. This fish is universally known simply as 'Platy', which is an abbreviation of the scientific name *Platypoecilus maculatus*, bestowed on it by its discoverer Günther in 1866. The scientific name has subsequently been changed. The male can be distinguished from the female by its anal fin which has been modified into a gonopodium; unlike the previous species, the male Platy does not have an extended lower caudal fin. This fish is ovoviviparous with a monthly reproductive cycle, and if the ripe and well-fed females are isolated in large tanks, generations of 30–100 fry can be obtained. The female also has cannibal instincts and if the fry are to be completely saved she should be placed in a breeding cage (which can be obtained from specialist shops) so that the fry can escape her. The wild strains have very many variations in colouring. Through selective breeding many strains of red, green, yellow and black have been obtained. The fish in plate 49 is a red female Wagtail Platy, so called by its discoverer Gordon, who obtained this through a particular cross. It is uniformly red with blackish fins. It has been observed that two species, *Xiphophorus helleri* and *Xiphophorus maculatus* can be crossed, giving a fecund hybrid (plate 48) with the characteristics of both parents. For example, the two fish in plate 50 (male left, female right) are probably hybrids

obtained from a green Swordtail and a red Platy like the one in plate 49.

51 Three-spot Gourami, *Trichogaster trichopterus* (Palas). Comes from the large Indonesian islands of Malacca, and from Thailand and Vietnam. It is a very beautiful fish which quickly reaches its maximum length of 15 cm. It is suitable for aquariums of 22°–28°C containing other medium-sized fish. The Cosby (plate 51) is a popular variety, commonly known in Italy as Gorgonzola Fish because its marbled appearance is very reminiscent of the famous cheese. To breed, a female, distinguishable by her small and rounded dorsal fin, and a male should be placed in a tank full of plants. The eggs are deposited in a nest made of air bubbles and hundreds of fry are hatched from them.

52 Dwarf Gourami, *Colisa lalia* (Hamilton-Buchanan). Originating in India, this is the smallest fish (a maximum length of 5 cm) of its kind. The male is very beautifully coloured, as can be seen from the photograph, and although it is delicate, it is a popular acquisition. The aquarium temperature should be between 22°–28°C. Like the other fish of the Anabantid family (*Trichogaster, Betta, Macropodus, Helostoma*, etc) it possesses 'feelers', auxiliary respiratory organs situated above the gill chambers (one on each side) which allow it to breathe atmospheric air. For this reason it can survive in water which is only slightly oxygenated. During the breeding period the parent fish prepare a nest of air bubbles attached to floating plants; after the eggs have been spawned the female should immediately be taken away from the male as she will attack him vigorously.

53

54

55

53-4 Siamese Fighting Fish, *Betta splendens* (Regan). Found in slow-flowing waterways in Thailand and the Malacca Peninsula. This fish too has auxiliary respiratory organs which allow it to make use of atmospheric air and it does not therefore need oxygen from the water. In its natural state this famous fighting fish will grow to 5 cm in length but in captivity, at a temperature of 22°–28°C, it is bigger and its colours are more brilliant and iridescent. By selective breeding its aggressive instincts have been increased. When two males confront each other (plate 53) their colours become more sombre, they spread out their fins and raise the membranes of the gill covers; when fighting they tear each other's fins off, but fortunately they grow again in 10–20 days. In an aquarium there should obviously be only one male; indeed, if he sees his reflection in a mirror he will immediately assume an aggressive attitude. The female (plate 54) is more modestly garbed and is kept for breeding purposes. The male prepares a nest of air bubbles in which the pair deposit the eggs, which he tends exclusively.

55-6 Paradise Fish, *Macropodus opercularis* (Linnaeus). Found in Korea, China and Formosa. It is very hardy and will tolerate drops in temperature. Generally it is only young fish that are sold (plate 56) but not until its adult state does it develop fins and those colours which justly give it its name Paradise Fish. The albino variety (plate 55) is very common.

56

57

57 Kissing Gourami, *Helostoma temmincki* (Cuvier and Valenciennes). This fish is found in the waters of Thailand, Malacca, Sumatra, Borneo and Java. It is fished for food, as its flesh is greatly appreciated. While in its natural state it can grow to a fairly large size (30 cm), in an aquarium at a temperature of 23°–28°C it is considerably smaller. However it should always be kept with fish which are not much smaller than it is. It should be fed twice a day, dried food being alternated with *Tubifex* or something similar. It is commonly known as a Kissing Gourami because of its strange behaviour: every so often two fish will press their mouths one to the other and in this position they will float like two lovers in a tender embrace. Usually it is two males which come together but the significance of this behaviour is not known. Identification of sex is purely by the swollen belly of the female. During spawning the female lays many eggs which float in the water; sometimes the parents eat the eggs, but they spare whatever fry are hatched.

58 Green Puffer Fish, *Tetraodon fluviatilis* (Hamilton-Buchanan). This species is distributed in the fresh and brackish waters of Thailand, Malacca, Sumatra,

Java, Borneo, the Philippines and India. To enable it to adapt to aquarium life it is advisable to add 1–2 teaspoons of salt to every 10 litres of water and to feed it with a diet of grubs (*Tubifex*) and small aquatic snails. In its natural state it will break the shell of molluscs with its strong teeth, and grows to a considerable size (15 cm). In an aquarium only smaller fish of this type are kept because the adult will often eat other fish. They are variously coloured with dark spots scattered over their backs, and greenish yellow on their flanks. When this fish is frightened it will defend itself by puffing itself up beyond its normal size and raising the small dermal spine covering its body. The same phenomenon can be observed if the fish is taken out of water and placed on the hand: it puffs up like a balloon.

59 Puffer Fish, *Tetraodon palembangensis* (Bleeker). Another Puffer Fish which lives in the fresh waters of Thailand, Borneo and Sumatra. Compared with the last, this species has more pronounced dermal spines and a more decorative colouring.

58

59

60

61

62

60 Black-banded Sunfish, *Mesogonistius chaetodon* (Baird). One of the most beautiful of the sunfish, it is straw yellow with various irregular, black transverse bands. It is found in eastern United States (from Florida to New Jersey). Its maximum length is 8–10 cm and it is ideal for the novice aquarist who does not like complications. Living at 10°–20°C it can be reared in a normal tank without special heating and will reproduce easily. In the reproductive period the belly of the female is very swollen and she is more intensely coloured. This is when she should be isolated with a male, in a tank into which has been put some synthetic cotton fibre or many-branched aquatic plants with small leaves. The fry are cared for by the male, and after she has spawned the female should be removed.

61 Indian Glassfish, *Chanda ranga* (Hamilton-Buchanan). Originating in India, this fish has been bred in other parts of the world for sale in tropical fish shops. More commonly known by aquarists under its other name, *Ambassis lala*, it is a small, pretty fish, perfectly transparent. Its natural surroundings are fresh and brackish water. In an aquarium at a temperature of 20°–25°C it is advisable to add 3–4 teaspoons of kitchen salt for every 10 litres of water. Its surroundings should be very well lit, with plenty of vegetation and dried food which can be alternated with grubs and small brine shrimps. It breeds easily but the fry nearly always die of starvation as it is difficult to feed them.

62 Finger Fish or Malay Angelfish, *Monodactylus argenteus* (Linnaeus). This species is widely diffused, from Polynesia to East Africa, in both fresh and sea water. It adapts well to fresh water at 23°–28°C with 3–4 teaspoons of salt added for every 10 litres of water. Its body is discus-shaped, a delicate pale silvery yellow in colour. It is very lively and therefore suitable only for aquariums of at least 30 litres.

63

63 Argus Fish, Leopard Scat, *Scatophagus argus* (Linnaeus). Lives in fresh and salt water in the Indo-Pacific regions. Its body is slim and discus-like with a bilobular dorsal fin, supported by spines. Its colour varies, normally yellow bronze with round black spots which sometimes blend into irregular vertical bands. This fish can, in its natural state, reach a length of 30 cm, but in a normal aquarium it rarely reaches half that length. It should be kept at a temperature of 24°–30°C and the water should be slightly salty (4 teaspoons of kitchen salt to every 10 litres of fresh water). Initially it should be fed on live food but later it will eat almost any type of food, as well as anything edible it finds in the aquarium – including fish excrement. Its diet should be enriched with vegetables (lettuce) so that it does not devour all the aquatic plants. The name *Scatophagus* signifies eater of excrement, and this name was given to it after all kinds of filth had been found in the intestines of fish caught near inhabited areas. It is very welcome in an aquarium on account of its peaceful nature (it can be trusted even with tiny guppies) and its habits which are comparable with the very beautiful fish found in coral reefs.

64 Tiger Scat, *Scatophagus argus*. A variety of the Argus Fish with a more lively colouring enhanced by red spots on the back.

65 Golden Lake Malawi Cichlid, *Pseudotropheus auratus* (Boulenger). This species lives in Lake Malawi (Africa) and has only recently been imported. It is a fish with an aerodynamic shape, 8–10 cm long, which should be kept in a fairly large aquarium with fish of its own size, as it is very lively and sometimes aggressive. The water temperature should be between 23°–28°C. Diet, which could be an alternation of vegetable and animal food, is not a problem as this fish adapts easily. Its colouring is striking, the colours similar in their softness to those of other coral fish. The bodies of some young fish are golden yellow with black horizontal stripes, one of which passes through the eye; the tail is spotted with black. The sexes can only be distinguished when the fish are adult: the male is very dark on the lower half of his body and the female is pale and her dorsal fin is edged with black. The fertilised eggs are kept in the mouth of the mother fish where they hatch. The fry are kept in their mother's mouth until they are well developed.

64

65

66
67

66 Red-finned Cichlid, *Labeotropheus trewavasae* (Fryer). Like the previous species, this one lives in Lake Malawi where it reaches 10 cm in length. It has similar habits and should be housed in a large aquarium at 23°–28°C with fish of medium size. Its normal diet is dried food, so lettuce or spinach should be added. With its mouth gently inclined towards the bottom this fish cleans objects covered with algae. The male is predominantly blue with slight vertical bars of a darker blue and a red dorsal fin. The female has a chestnut colouring, less striking.

67 Flag Cichlid, *Aequidens curviceps* (Ahl). Found in the Amazon, its maximum length is 8 cm. In a large aquarium full of plants and at a temperature of 23°–28°C this pleasant and timid fish adapts very well, and unlike other Cichlids it does not destroy the aquatic plants. The adult fish have long anal and dorsal fins (particularly the males); their colouring varies. These fish breed as follows: the mating pair, isolated in an aquarium full of vegetation, will spend hours on end looking for a suitable spot to deposit the eggs. Having chosen this, they then clean it thoroughly with their mouths, and the female emits an egg-laying organ (ovipositor) with which the eggs are expelled and immediately fertilised by the male. Very occasionally the parents will eat their eggs but usually they are occupied in tending the fry which are hatched 3–4 days later. In these early phases of spawning and hatching the aquarium should be as quiet as possible: if they are frightened the parents will immediately devour the fry.

68 69

68-9 Angelfish, *Pterophyllum eimekei* (Ahl) and *Pterophyllum scalare* (Lichtenstein). These two species, very similar, live in the Amazon and Rio Negro basins where they can grow to quite a large size (15 cm long and 25 cm high). It is difficult to distinguish between the two species, and indeed the distinction is based on the number of spines in the dorsal and anal fins, and the rows of scales which run from the gill cover to the base of the caudal stem. To make things more complicated one can often buy hybrids which have been obtained from interbreeding the two species. Because of their shape they are commonly known as Angelfish or Scalare. The body, almost discoidal, is flat and has tall, uneven fins. Several black bands (4–6), more or less complete, furrow the shimmering nacreous body. An aquarium (temperature 22°–30°C) is embellished by these beautiful tenants which do, however, eat smaller fish. They can be found in different shades of black (Black Angelfish) and with very long fins (Lacetail). These latter have very delicate fins which break easily in transport and in contact with other more vivacious fish. It is comparatively rare to find a specimen with perfect fins, such as the one in plate 68.

70 Angelfish are very timid and live best in shoals. They are, however, very sensitive to any lowering of the oxygen level of the water and for this reason an aerator should always be in use. In breeding, the difficulty is to find a pair which have an 'affinity' for each other. The sexes can be distinguished only during the mating season, when the male emits a conical genital papilla and the female a cylindrical genital papilla. Unfortunately, having chosen a pair from which to breed, there is no guarantee that they will do so. From this point of view Angelfish are very demanding and it is best to wait for spontaneous pairing which tends to separate them from the other fish. The pair are then isolated in a large well-lit tank at 26°C with plenty of vegetation and live food (*Tubifex, Artemia,* etc). With the greatest tranquillity the two fish thoroughly clean a small area of the tank wall and a plant with large leaves, remove any refuse and the filter of algae and then deposit the fertilised and adhesive eggs. The parents tend the eggs carefully: they stir the water with their fins to oxygenate it, clean the eggs and finally, after 2–3 days, help the fry to hatch. Usually 500–1000 fish are hatched and remain suspended in the water for a time attached to the leaves by mucous filaments, carefully tended by their parents. After the first spawning the parents will remain together until death.

71

72

71 Firemouth, *Cichlasoma meeki* (Brind). Found from Yucatan to Guatemala. Because of its aggressive instincts this fish (13–15 cm long) should in its adult state be kept only in an aquarium with other fish of the same size; water temperature should be 20°–28°C. It should be fed mostly on live food. As can be seen from the photograph, the young fish has a muted colouring; the mature fish is generally violet blue interspersed with transverse bands and with a blue mask on its nose. Characteristic of this species is the smudge edged with green at the base of the gill cover, and the bright red colouring which extends along the belly and the lower part of the head: these give it its popular name of Firemouth. To breed from these fish, a mature male, identifiable by its long and pointed dorsal fin, should be selected. The difficulty is to find the right pair, after which in a properly tended aquarium spawning will occur naturally, and many fry be hatched.

72 Festive Cichlid, *Chichlasoma festivum* (Heckel). This species is widely found in the fresh waterways of Guyana and in the Amazon and Rio Negro basins. Only young specimens should be put into an aquarium which has many different varieties of fish. Adult fish (up to 15 cm long) should be put with larger fish. They need strongly oxygenated water and a temperature of 20°–28°C. This fish is easily distinguishable from other Cichlids by the black stripe which starts at the mouth, passes through the eye and continues down the length of the body to the extreme tip of the dorsal fin. Distinctions between the sexes and breeding habits are similar to the preceding species; during this period the pair should not be disturbed.

73 Marble, Oscar or Velvet Cichlid, *Astronotus ocellatus* (Cuvier). Found in Guyana, Venezuela and in the Amazon and Paraguay basins. It can grow to a considerable length (30 cm) and although it is aggressive towards smaller fish it is much prized by aquarists for its intelligence and behaviour: it seems to be able to recognise the people who look after it. The temperature of the aquarium should be 23°–28°C. It is a voracious fish which likes large pieces of fish, meat, molluscs and small live fish. Its body is olive brown with a faint stippling of orange and red spots, particularly noticeable in male and adult fish. Like almost all other Cichlids, *Astronotus* deposits a lot of eggs which, if it does not devour, it tends carefully.

74 Jewel Cichlid, *Hemichromis bimaculatus* (Gill). Very common in tropical Africa (in the Rivers Nile, Congo and Niger), this is a strong and lively fish, not suitable for an aquarium containing other fish. Water temperature should be 22°–28°C. This fish is identifiable by its two black spots, one on the flank under the dorsal fin and the other above the gill cover. The young fish (photographed) is not brightly coloured. During the mating season the adult male (10–15 cm long) becomes red with blue spots scattered over its body. Generally it is the male which is more brilliantly coloured, but during the mating season it is the female. Their breeding habits are the same as other Cichlids. The early mating moves should be carefully watched, however, because if the female is not ready to spawn the male may attack and possibly kill her.

75 Niger Cichlid, *Pelmatochromis kribensis* (Boulenger). This species comes from the tropical regions of West Africa. It is much sought after because it is a peaceful fish which likes to hide in the vegetation. It needs a temperature of 24°–30°C. The male is larger than the female (8–9 cm long to her 6–7 cm) and its colouring more brilliant. To breed, the mating pair should be put in an aquarium with plenty of aquatic plants and some large shells, placed so that they can be used as a hiding place; the pair will deposit the eggs under these. It is a good idea to remove the pair after the eggs have been deposited, because sometimes they are inclined to devour them.

76

76 Bumblebee Fish or Wasp Goby, *Brachygobius xanthozona* (Bleeker). Found in Java, Borneo and Sumatra. It is 4–5 cm long, docile, and can be kept in a normal tropical aquarium at a temperature of 23°–26°C. Its colouring is yellow tending towards orange, usually with four transverse maroon bands which run through the fins. A characteristic of this fish is the clear yellow stripe which bisects the first two bands. Breeding: the aquarium should be a large one with plenty of hiding places made of stones and large shells where the eggs will be deposited. The male, which looks after the eggs, is identifiable by its more marked colouring and slimmer profile.

77 Brine Shrimp (young), *Artemia salina* (Linnaeus). A small marine crustacean with a very high nutritive value, it is an essential diet for fry. One can buy *Artemia* eggs and they should be treated as follows: take a shallow, 3–5 litre container with plenty of surface area, fill it with fresh water and add

kitchen salt (2 teaspoons of salt for every litre of fresh water); to this add a pinch of the eggs and mix well together. After 2–3 days at a temperature of 20°–26°C the eggs hatch (on the left of the photograph, enlarged 100 times) and very small larvae (*nauplii*) emerge (right, same enlargement). These can be extracted with a siphon, filtered through a fine sieve and fed to the fish.

78 Cuprina Snail, *Pomacea bridgesi diffusa* (Blume). This large aquarium mollusc which sometimes has a spiral shell, inaccurately but commonly known as Cuprina, is found in the fresh waters of tropical regions. It is useful for cleaning the aquarium, feeding mainly on algae, vegetation and dead fish. It can lead an amphibious life as it has both gill and lung cavities. It often rises to the surface and takes in air through a long inhalatory siphon. If several are kept in one aquarium they will often deposit masses of very hard, reddish-yellow eggs around the edges, out of the water, from which emerge hundreds of *Pomaceae*.

77

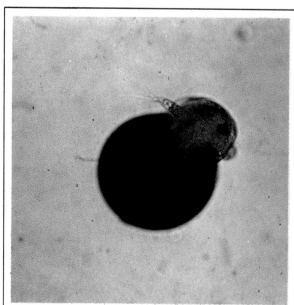
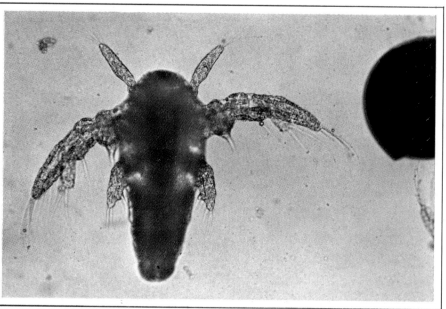

79-80 Pond Turtles or Terrapins can be kept in fresh-water aquariums which they will greatly enliven. Young specimens of Red-eared Terrapins *Pseudemys scripta troostii* (Gray) and *Pseudemys scripta elegans*, for example, are imported from Florida. These are vividly coloured with stripes of green and yellow on the head and limbs. Also on the head, behind the eye, there is a bright red spot. The shell is variously patterned and coloured. They have pulmonary respiration and must therefore continually rise to the surface to breathe, but they can swim below the water for long periods without breathing. They are useful because they tend to attack and devour sick fish which are unable to escape. However, when they reach a length of 5 cm they should be isolated in a suitable tank. They should be fed on *Tubifex* and special foods rich in calcelareous substances since a lack of calcium in their diet causes a softening of the shell. It is a good idea to provide the aquarium with a partly submerged rock so that the turtle can live out of the water.

81 In a salt-water aquarium other interesting organisms beside fish can be kept. Among these are Hermit Crabs, small crustaceans with chelae (claws) with which they seize their food, for the most part dead fish, pieces of meat and other animal products. Unlike crayfish they have a soft belly and are therefore vulnerable to attacks from predators. To defend themselves they crawl into discarded mollusc shells which they drag with them wherever they go. In some cases one or two anemones (plate 81 shows a commensal anemone *Caliactis parasitica* on a Hermit Crab's shell) will attach themselves to the shell, where they will live symbiotically, symbiosis being a mutually beneficial association between two different organisms. The Hermit Crab is camouflaged and defended by the anemone, which keeps other animals at bay by means of sting capsules attached to its tentacles. At the same time, the anemone, attached to the shell, is able more easily to capture food; it will normally eat what the Hermit Crab discards. When the Hermit Crab grows too large for the shell it abandons it and finds a larger one, but it takes the anemone with it (in its claws) and attaches it to its new home.

82 Butterfly Fish, *Heniochus acuminatus*. This is a fish from the coral reefs of the Indian and Pacific Oceans. It is fished for its flesh which is very tasty. It can be reared, with other fish, in a marine aquarium at a temperature of 26°–30°C, feeding on worms, brine shrimps and dried food. Its body is silvery, interspersed with two broad, brown, almost black, transverse stripes. The pectoral, dorsal and caudal fins are yellow: more accurately, the front of the dorsal fin is white and elongated to form a long crest.

82

83 Trigger Fish, *Balistapus undulatus* (Mungo Park). Very common in Polynesia and Japan, it is widely found in tropical seas, living on molluscs whose shells it breaks with its powerful mouth. This species is one of the Crossbow or Trigger Fish, so called on account of the first few spines of the dorsal fin: the first long spine, when it is erect, cannot be folded back again without displacing all the others, which function like the safety catch on a rifle.

84 Angelfish, *Pomacanthus sp*. These are very welcome in a marine aquarium for their dazzling colours. Their markings and colouring will vary according to their age. *Pomacanthus semicirculatus* and *Pomacanthus imperator*, for example, when young are blue with thin white curving stripes, while in their adult state their markings and colourings are completely different. In *Pomacanthus imperator* the stripes turn yellow and are almost horizontal.

85 Clown Fish, *Amphiprion percula* (Bleeker). Lives in the Indian and Pacific Oceans in company with large sea anemones. Unlike other fish which fear the sting capsules of these anemones, the Clown Fish, when it senses danger, hides among these tentacles without being stung – on the contrary it will rub itself freely against them. It gets its name of Clown Fish from its colouring: orange with three white rings, one around its head, one around the middle of the body and the third around the caudal stem. These rings are so clearly drawn that they could have been done by hand.

85

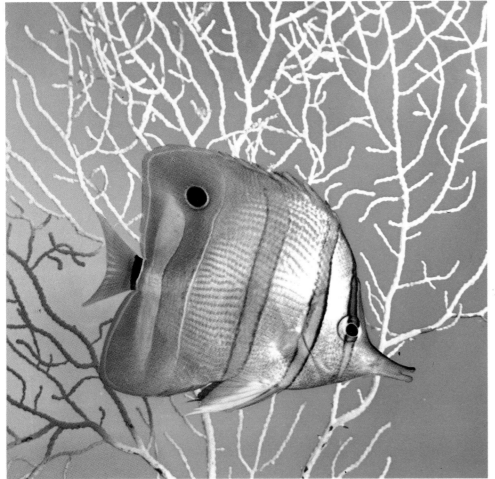

86 Trunkfish, Boxfish, *Ostracion sp*. These fish
live in the tropical regions of the Pacific, Atlantic
and Indian Oceans. They are commonly known as
Trunk- or Boxfish on account of the unusual
prismatic shape of their body, which is clad in a
mosaic of bony plates fused together to form a
solid carapace. The *Ostracion* in the inset
photograph is taken from an angle which clearly
shows its shape, reminiscent of a box. The result is
an extremely rigid body with freedom of movement
restricted to the eyes, mouth and fins. It swims
slowly by moving its dorsal and caudal fins.
Normally it lies on the bottom of the aquarium. It
will feed on small animals which it tears from the
rocks with its strong teeth. The rigidity of its body
hampers its respiration, which is why it moves its
pectoral fins vigorously, directing a current of
oxygenated water towards its gills. It is not
advisable to keep these fish with other species
because if they are suddenly startled or angry they
will emit a poisonous substance which is lethal for
other inhabitants of the aquarium.

87 Longnose Butterfly Fish, *Chelmon rostratus*
(Cuvier). This is an Indo-Pacific species from
northern Australia to Mauritius which, when
young, will adapt easily to marine aquarium life,
eating live food (*Tubifex, Artemia salina*). Its
profile is unusual: it has an elongated beak-like
mouth with which it will search out small creatures
hidden in holes and crevices in the rocks. Its body
is silvery with five vertical orange stripes, the first of
which passes through the eye while the penultimate
spreads out on to the caudal fin, isolating a round
black spot. This fish has the habit of rising to the
surface and emitting minute jets of water from its
mouth – perhaps to trap small insects; it was once
confused with the Archerfish.

88 Wrasse, *Thalassoma lunare*. This tropical wrasse is found in coral formations. It has a green elongated body with a varying pattern of violet which is particularly noticeable on its head and fins. There is a large yellow spot on its tail. It is a powerful fish which is best kept on its own in an aquarium; it should be fed chiefly with live food (*Tubifex*, *Artemia salina*).

89 Butterfly Fish, *Chaetodon sp*. This lives among coral reefs in tropical seas; it is particularly admired for its brilliant colouring, its strange shape and elegant movements which are common to the greater part of the Chaetodontid family. As in all the butterfly fish, its body is compressed, and it has a small pouting mouth provided with teeth, with which it extracts the prey it finds in the crevices and detritus of coral reefs.

88

89